pharmakon

Quentin Meillassoux

pharmakon

SCIENCE FICTION AND EXTRO-SCIENCE FICTION

followed by "The Billiard Ball" by Isaac Asimov

Translated by Alyosha Edlebi   UNIVOCAL

Métaphysique et fiction des mondes hors-science
by Quentin Meillassoux
© 2013 Éditions Aux forges de Vulcain

Translated by Alyosha Edlebi
as *Science Fiction and Extro-Science Fiction*

First Edition
Minneapolis © 2015, Univocal Publishing

Published by Univocal
123 North 3rd Street, #202
Minneapolis, MN 55401

Thanks to Robyn Asimov, Suhail Malik,
Robin Mackay, and Grace Kavanah

Designed & Printed by Jason Wagner
Distributed by the University of Minnesota Press

ISBN 9781937561482

Library of Congress Control Number 2015936112

Science Fiction and Extro-Science Fiction

Science Fiction and Extro-Science Fiction[1]

I would like to elaborate, throughout the course of this text, a difference between two regimes of fiction that strikes me as metaphysically significant. These two regimes concern experimental sciences; to designate them, I will use two names, one of which is well-known and the other is a neologism: science fiction, on the one hand; and on the other, what I call "extro-science fiction,"[2] or in shorthand: SF and XSF.

Before explaining this difference, I would like to introduce a clarification in order to avoid misunderstandings and potential objections. I will propose a definition of science fiction that is rather common and banal, in order to clearly distinguish it from

---

1. A shorter version of this text was initially presented on May 18, 2006, at the "Metaphysics and Science Fiction" conference at the École normale supérieure (Paris-Ulm).
2. Fictions (des mondes) hors-science.

what I call extro-science fiction. But once I have defined these two notions, you will perhaps think that the literary genre called science fiction also contains extro-science fictions, that there are examples of XSF novels in SF and therefore that the literary genre SF contradicts the distinction I am maintaining. My aim is not to contest this point; rather, it is to underscore a conceptual distinction and to show its philosophical import. Starting from here, two things are possible: either no XSF novels exist in futuristic literature, and the genre itself of "science fiction" confirms the proposed conceptual difference; or such novels do exist. In the second case then, my thesis is that these XSF novels—even though they are inscribed in the SF genre—do not belong to science fiction, but to a profoundly different regime of fiction and should as such be singularized: they constitute, in some sense, a "genre within the genre," an "empire within the empire."

1. Science Fiction and Extro-Science Fiction

Let's examine this difference: science fiction and extro-science fiction.

Generally speaking, in science fiction the relation of fiction to science seems to be the following: it is a matter of imagining a fictional future of science that modifies, and often expands, its possibilities of knowledge and mastery of the real. Man's relation to the world undergoes a change by virtue of a modification to scientific knowledge, which opens up unheard-of possibilities for him. Whatever upheavals the possible futures introduce, they necessarily stand—at the heart of science fiction—within the orbit of science. Every science fiction implicitly maintains the following axiom: in the anticipated future it will *still* be possible to subject the world to a scientific knowledge. Science will be transfigured by its new power, but it will always exist. Hence, of course, the generic name to designate this type of literature: fiction can produce extreme variations, but at the heart of it a science is always present, albeit in an unrecognizable form.

Now, what do we mean by "fiction of worlds outside-science," namely extro-science fiction or "XSF?" By the term "extro-science world," we are not referring to worlds that are simply devoid of science, i.e., worlds in which experimental sciences do not in fact exist. For example: worlds in which human beings have not, or have not yet, developed a scientific relation to the real. By extro-science worlds we mean worlds where, *in principle, experimental science is impossible* and not unknown *in fact*. Extro-science fiction thus defines a particular regime of the imaginary in which structured—or rather destructured—worlds are conceived in such a way that experimental science cannot deploy its theories or constitute its objects within them. The guiding question of extro-science fiction is: what should a world be, what should a world resemble, so that it is in principle inaccessible to a scientific knowledge, so that it cannot be established as the object of a natural science?

My aim, throughout the course of this text, is to provide a precise conceptual content to this still very general and simply negative definition of extro-science worlds. At the same time, I will try to show the properly speculative benefit of becoming aware of the difference between science fiction and extro-science fiction and, on the other hand, of cultivating XSF, this type of imaginary that is distinct from SF.

Why do I raise such questions? If I am interested in extro-science fiction, it is because this fiction is the source of a very classical metaphysical problem to which I have devoted myself for a long time, namely the problem of induction. Or more precisely: the problem of the necessity of the laws of nature in the way Hume posits it in *Treatise of Human Nature*, and later on in *Enquiry on Human Understanding*. This problem, whose nature I will recall in a moment, was profoundly misunderstood by one of the most important epistemologists of the 20th century: Karl Popper. In fact, Popper boasted of having been the first to designate the problem of induction with the expression "Hume's Problem," and he claimed to bring a rigorous and original response to this problem. I want to begin by showing that Popper's failure to understand Hume stems precisely from the fact that he conflated a problem of XSF with a problem of SF. Popper did not raise the same problem as Hume; in my opinion he mobilized another type of imaginary, because if Hume mobilizes the imaginary of extro-science fiction to pose his problem, the problem Popper raised can only be conceived by means of a science fiction imaginary.

Next, I will examine Kant's response to Hume's problem found in the *Critique of Pure Reason*, and more precisely in the "Objective Deduction of the Categories." In contrast to Popper, Kant was not mistaken about the nature of Hume's problem; he responded to it on its proper terrain, the one that consists in "fictioning" a world in which science has become impossible. But I will equally critique Kant's thesis, by demonstrating that the weakness of the transcendental deduction stems in particular from an insufficiently developed imaginary of extro-science—an imaginary that is too restricted in some sense. I will then show that a more acute sense of extro-science fiction allows us to extract a third response to Hume's problem, distinct from both Popper's and Kant's.

2. Two Billiard Games: Hume and Asimov

a) Formulation of the Problem

The most celebrated of Hume's writings where he poses the problem of causal necessity consists of a description of an imaginary billiard game, in the course of which the laws of collision cease to hold. Here is the relevant passage from *Enquiry on Human Understanding*:

> When I see, for instance, a billiard-ball moving in a straight line towards another; even suppose motion in the second ball should not by accident be suggested to me, as the result of their contact or impulse; may I not conceive, that a hundred different events might as well follow from that cause? May not both these balls remain at absolute rest? May not the first ball return in a straight line, or leap off from the second in any line or direction? All these suppositions are consistent and conceivable. Why then should we give the preference to one, which is no more consistent or conceivable than the rest? All our reasonings *a priori* will never be able to show us any foundation for this preference.[3]

---

3. David Hume, *An Enquiry Concerning Human Understanding; and Other Writings*, ed. Stephen Buckle (Cambridge University Press, 2007), 32.

In these imaginary scenes, the question Hume poses consists in knowing what exactly guarantees for us—but also what convinces us—that physical laws will still be valid in the next moment, since neither experience nor logic can give us such an assurance. For there is no logical contradiction in imagining that the laws will be modified in the future, and no experience of past constancy allows us to infer that they will endure in the future. On the one hand, it is in fact not contradictory for nature to obey up to time t a certain number of physical constancies and to stop obeying them at time $t + 1$. An entity is contradictory only if it is at the same time, and according to the same aspect, a and *non-a*. But if an entity is in state a (nature subject to known laws) and *then* in state *non-a* (nature not subject to known laws), logic cannot find any fault with it. So we cannot, in the name of logical coherence, refute *a priori* the hypothesis according to which nature could begin to obey constancies other than those already identified. If we cannot refute a hypothesis *a priori* (that is, independently of experience, by pure reasoning), we can still attempt to refute it *a posteriori*, i.e., by an appeal to experience. However, experience by definition can only tell us about the present (what I am experiencing now) and about the past (what I have already experienced); there is no experience of the future. How can we then ground within experience the certainty that tomorrow nature will obey the known constancies it obeys today? It will no doubt be objected that science allows us to predict with precision a certain number of future phenomena—like the eclipse anticipated by the astronomer—and that these predictions have been confirmed numerous times in numerous domains, and this fact grounds, in reason, our confidence about predictions that have yet to be confirmed. But such predictions always rest on the hypothesis that current laws will be the same as the laws to come, precisely the point that has to be demonstrated. Even if natural laws have remained constant up until now (and only the theories that deal with these laws have evolved, not their intrinsic reality), nothing in experience—which is, once again, always present or past—can assure us this will always be the case. Nothing allows me to be certain that nature will not, soon, at this very moment, start doing just about anything, as in the Humean billiard game, defying every theory and every possible experience. Nothing except "good sense," one will perhaps say. But what should we make of a "good sense" that relies neither on logic nor on experience?

Thus the question that arises is knowing whether our certainty about a stable nature is justified and—failing that—understanding where this subjective assurance comes from that allows us to be so perfectly confident, on a daily basis, of the future constancy of the real. As we know, Hume believed that only the *habit* of past empirical constancies can persuade us that the future will resemble the past, without there being anything rational at the foundation of this judgment. In other words, instead of proving that there is indeed a causal necessity, the skeptical philosopher confines himself to uncovering the psychological source of our certainty that such a necessity exists. This solution did not satisfy those who, after Hume, attempted to resolve in their turn this challenge to reason—mainly Kant, then Karl Popper.

Let's begin with the most recent solution, Popper's, as put forward in his famous work *The Logic of Scientific Discovery*, and pursued further in his later works.

In principle, this solution is very simple. If we were to ask Popper what it is that guarantees that the Humean billiard ball will not adopt the aforementioned fantastical behaviors, not only would he have to respond that nothing can guarantee this but, furthermore, that this is a good thing because such a possibility has nothing fantastical about it and should be taken quite seriously. For Popper, in fact, our predictions about the future consist of theoretical hypotheses that are essentially falsifiable by new experiments, i.e., experiments that have not yet been identified. What makes a theory scientific, according to Popper, is precisely the fact that it can in principle be refuted experimentally. It is this intrinsic falsifiability of scientific conjectures that explains the dynamism of experimental science, the incessant movement in the course of which physicists advance new hypotheses, refute the old ones, and subject the competing theories to relentless tests. Affirming this, Popper opposes "inductivism," which claims to establish the definitive truth of a theory by multiplying its empirical "verifications." In truth, whatever the number of experimental verifications to which we submit a theory, it can always be refuted by a new experiment and can be surpassed by a new, more powerful theory that draws a novel chart of physical possibilities. It is thus not possible to affirm "in the name of physics" that such and such an event is definitively impossible: it is impossible only in the current state of science, without us ever being able to anticipate the future.

Consequently it is useless to ask (as Hume or the empiricists after him) what convinces us that the sun will rise tomorrow, that every living being will end up dying, or that bread nourishes. Nothing can, or must, persuade us of this, for the simple reason that it is not necessary. Moreover, this has not always been the case.

In *Objective Knowledge*, Popper affirms that the three examples of "established laws" are effectively refutable: the law according to which the sun will set once every twenty four hours was refuted by Pytheas of Marseilles when he discovered in polar regions "the frozen sea and the midnight sun"; the law according to which every living being has to perish was refuted "by the discovery that bacteria are not bound to die, since multiplication by fission is not death"; the law according to which bread nourishes (one of Hume's favorite examples) was refuted the day "people eating daily bread died of ergotism."[4]

If we return to the billiard balls, we should then say, following Popper, that they could adopt unexpected behaviors in the future, either because we can modify the circumstances of the experiment—for example, by metalizing them and introducing a powerful magnetic field—or because we will one day discover some means of modifying the gravitational field in which these balls evolve, with the help of scientific advances that are, for the moment, beyond our reach.

This is then the principle of Popper's solution to Hume's problem: every event, as unusual as it might appear to be, is compatible in principle with the current or future state of science. No event can therefore

4. Karl Popper, *Objective Knowledge* (Oxford University Press, 1972), 10-11.

be excluded in the name of reason, whether it be the reason of logic or the reason of experimental science.

Now, why did I say that such a solution amounted to a misinterpretation of the real problem formulated in *Enquiry on Human Understanding*? Let's note, first of all, that the Popperian solution moves entirely within an imaginary that is homogeneous to that of science fiction. In fact, what does falsificationism ask us to accept about scientific theory? Namely, that in the future such theories will perhaps be refuted in favor of other theories, which have not yet been envisioned. The examples Popper provides of such refutations obviously belong to the past, but the principle of his epistemology consists in projecting, into the future, the possibility of ruptures as radical as those that have already been produced and that saw, for example, Newtonian dynamics become obsolete in favor of theories as revolutionary as general relativity or quantum physics, which the men of the 18th century could not have anticipated. Even if we cannot know or even glimpse what the physics or biology of the future can be, we should accept the possibility of an experimental science to come that will be as dissimilar from current science as current science is from the science of past centuries. In order to access Popperian epistemology, it is purely and simply a matter of envisioning some indeterminate science fiction, because instead of inventing the positive content of the science of the future, we will confine ourselves to positing the possibility that such a content to come is wholly other than our current knowledge.

What then is Popper's misinterpretation of Hume? Popper poses, in reality, the following problem: can our *theories* be refuted in the future by new experiments? His problem is thus *epistemological*; it concerns the nature of scientific knowledge. But it is not *ontological*, in contrast to Hume's problem, which concerns not simply the stability of theories but the stability of *processes*, of physical laws themselves. Popper, via falsificationism, does not treat this ontological problem. He tells us in fact that new experiments can refute our theories; but he never doubts the fact that old and identified experiments will produce the same results in the future. In exactly identical circumstances, the same experiments will, according to him, always take place; only unprecedented circumstances can yield unprecedented results. We see this clearly in the proposed examples: it is only near the poles that the sun no longer rises every twenty-four hours, and it is only owing to a lethal fungus that bread transmits ergotism instead of nourishing. According to Popper, in unchanged circumstances we will never see the sun escape gravity to "take a tour" outside of the system that bears its name; we will never see bread identical in its composition, for no reason, become a poison for the one who partakes in its nourishment. If this were the case, we would no longer be dealing with a science that has to revolutionize its theories in order to adapt to unprecedented experiments, but with an experimental science that has become impossible as a result of the collapse of physical laws themselves. If, in identical circumstances, phenomena produced absolutely different effects, totally unforeseeable from one occasion to the next, then it is the very idea of verification or—according to Popper's term—"corroboration" of theories by the experimental method that will be abolished, because this idea always rests on the reproducibility of the same experiments in identical circumstances. In effect, scientific experimentation never proceeds from a unique observation that scientists accept because of the allegedly reliable character of the witness; it consists in the essential possibility that every laboratory has of reproducing the initial observation by following the same protocol. Even statistical laws rest on a certain constancy of the result, which allows us to verify, in identical conditions of experimentation, if not the same effect, at least the same series of probabilities for a range of effects that is itself stable. If you abolish every constancy in the results of an identical experiment, the principle of experimentation—the reproduction at will of the phenomenon under the same conditions—will collapse and with it the possibility of the natural sciences, whether their theories are deterministic or probabilistic.[5]

b) Professor Priss' Crime

This hypothesis of a world to come in which science itself would become impossible is Hume's real problem. Popper's problem—the assurance of our theories—is a problem of science fiction; it moves within a fiction which assumes that science will always be possible in the future. But Hume's problem mobilizes another imaginary, an imaginary of *extro-science fiction*, the fiction of a world that has become too chaotic to allow for a scientific theory (whatever it may be) to be applied to reality. And we see that this difference between two regimes of fiction—SF and XSF—involves real metaphysical stakes, since its misrecognition by Popper led him to conflate

---

5. In *Logic of the Scientific Discovery* (chap. X), Popper clearly marks the difference between his problem—namely, that theories can be "falsified by new experiments"—and another question that he calls "the immutability of natural processes." The last question concerns the possible modification of natural regularities and not of theories: it is thus, in our own terms, a question of Hume's *real* problem. Popper stresses that this question is not within the purview of falsificationism, but proceeds from a "metaphysical belief" without which it is difficult to conceive a "practical action." There is no better way to indicate that Popper's problem (the falsifiability of theories) never really treated the Humean question (the potential changeability of natural processes).

the epistemological problem that was his own with Hume's ontological problem.

To sum up the difference between Hume's problem and Popper's, let us return to the example of the billiard ball with fantastical trajectories. According to Hume, the question is: what guarantees that the ball will not adopt a trajectory that is not only unforeseen, but in principle unforeseeable, and which cannot be modeled because it escapes not merely every identified law but every identifiable law? According to Popper, it is instead: what guarantees that unprecedented circumstances, combined with unidentified laws, will not allow the ball in an undetermined future to take trajectories that our current knowledge cannot foresee, although in principle these trajectories can be foreseen by a future state of science? The first question stands outside the limits of science fiction; the second completely belongs to SF.

There is a text of science fiction that perfectly illustrates this difference—to such a degree that it seems to have been written for this purpose. It is a short story by Isaac Asimov entitled "The Billiard Ball." This short story is the last in a collection, *Asimov's Mysteries*, whose principle is to combine science fiction tales with detective mysteries. In "The Billiard Ball," Asimov recounts a possible assassination plotted by a genius of theoretical physics, a specialist of the theory of relativity, an assassination conducted by means of a billiard ball. As we will see, the whole plot rests on the unforeseen trajectory of a billiard ball; but the heart of this story is only meaningful if we understand this unforeseen character in the framework of Popper's problematic—thus within the orbit of the imaginary of science fiction—and not in the XSF framework of Hume's problematic.

Let's recall the storyline. The narrator, a science journalist, confesses in his personal notes that he suspects the greatest scientist of his time—professor James Priss—to be behind an assassination. He relates the following events: although more honored than any other scientist in his time, James Priss has always lived in the shadow of Edward Bloom, a companion of his youth and a classmate, who, although having no theoretical talent, proved to be a genius at applying the most abstract theories of his time, and in particular those of Priss. Bloom is a sort of super-Edison, whose practical inventions secured him wealth and renown, to the dismay of Priss, whose notoriety never surpassed the limited fame of professional scientists. An implicit rivalry and a sort of mutual jealousy developed between the two men, each secretly envying the type of recognition the other enjoys, a rivalry that crystallizes in the weekly billiard game that Priss and Bloom, two formidable players, have grown accustomed to playing since their youth.

This hostility, masked in civil and friendly guises, comes into the open when Bloom claims to apply Priss' theory to the antigravitaional field. In this theory, which earned him a second Nobel, Priss demonstrated the possibility of annulling every gravitational effect by opposing gravitation to an electromagnetic field capable of neutralizing its effects. Except that, according to Priss, this possibility, while true in theory, is impossible to realize in practice, because the electromagnetic field needed for this effect necessarily has to be infinite and is therefore technically unrealizable. Bloom challenges him and announces that he will succeed in producing an antigravity device without an infinite electromagnetic field. The discussion between the two becomes heated, and their reputations come into play in the matter; but after a year, Bloom announces that he has fulfilled his promise and invites the entire press to witness the first public demonstration of his success. He also perfidiously invites professor Priss to challenge the marvelous application of his brilliant theory in front of the world.

Once all the invitees are present, Bloom asks each of them to visit his laboratory where a stunning device awaits them. At the center of the room, crammed full of various devices, stands a billiard table, and at the center of this table a vertical light ray. Bloom offers the following explanation: he has never in fact tested his antigravific ray on a material object, even though he is certain it will function properly. He wanted Priss to have the honor of testing it by sending a billiard ball into the central ray. Here we have a supreme perversion that, in the guise of homage to a man of science, condemns him to ridicule himself before the whole world, by leaving to his rival the benefit of a billiard game that Priss will have lost forever. According to Bloom's predictions, the ball, weightless in the ray, will be seen to rise slowly along its length. All the participants are wearing sunglasses because of the light released by the ray, a fact that prevents them from seeing Priss' expression at the moment Bloom provides his explanation. At first paralyzed, Priss seems to pull himself together. He approaches the table and takes aim for a long time. The ball is struck; it adopts a complicated trajectory, bounces back, and then penetrates the light ray. A thunderous noise is heard; everyone is distraught; then, when the calm has returned, we discover Bloom dead, transpierced in the heart by the billiard ball.

A totally unforeseen event has thus taken place: the ball adopted a trajectory that is aberrant not only for our own physics, but also for the fictional physics of Priss and Bloom. If the story were Humean, i.e., extro-science fiction, there would be nothing more to say about this aberrant event, and the plot would leave us unsatisfied. But fortunately it is a story of science fiction, i.e., Popperian, and the plot finds a brilliant denouement. Priss finally explains in scientific terms the cause of the catastrophe, which he failed to foresee, since he is known to have always thought slowly. The explosion was due, he says, to the fact that an object detached from every gravitation cannot behave with the calm of the weightless object; it can only move at the speed of a massless object, i.e., the speed of a photon, the speed of light. And the story closes on the anxious interrogation of the narrator-journalist: what if, for once in his life, faced with the danger of seeing his reputation ruined in the eyes of everyone, Priss had understood at once what would happen, and took the time to calculate the trajectory required for the billiard ball to avenge him forever?

As you see, the story works because it is Popperian: it rests on the fact that the event, which is unforeseen in fact, was not unforeseen in principle, because a physical law can explain it. The crux of the story resides precisely in the possibility—which can never be proven—that Priss had effectively foreseen what would happen. The prediction has to be possible for the story to work; thus the event has to be subject to a theoretical law, but it will always be impossible to know whether the scientist had understood this law in time to commit his crime.

Beyond this story, a more general conclusion seems to emerge with respect to the literary value of the two regimes of fiction: namely, that only science fiction appears to permit the construction of a storyline, of a narration that is certainly fanciful but coherent. In fact, in science fiction we generally inhabit a world where physics (theoretical, natural) differs from ours, but in which laws are not purely and simply abolished—i.e., in which everything and anything cannot happen in an arbitrary way or at any moment. Stories can thus be told because we are still dealing with worlds, with ordered totalities, although they are governed by another order. Individuals can act within them—in this case, premeditate a murder—because they can always foresee the consequences of their actions within these worlds. In extro-science fiction, on the other hand, it seems that no order of any sort can be constituted and, therefore, no story can be told. If this were true, we would be wrong to speak of extro-science *worlds*, for a world incapable of giving place to science would no longer be a world but a pure chaos, a pure diversity that orders nothing. This is precisely Kant's thesis, and here we find its resolution of Hume's problem: if laws were not necessary, according to the *Critique of Pure Reason*, no world or any consciousness would emerge, nothing but a pure manifold without cohesion or development. We will try to show that we can challenge this thesis, because an extro-science world and even a plurality of worlds are in fact conceivable without "incoherence." We will thus try to legitimate both the metaphysical value of these worlds—by making them worlds whose possibility we cannot deny—as well as their literary value—by making them the possible setting of a fictional plot.

2. Transcendental Deduction and the Three Types of XSF Worlds

a) Kantian Rejection of the Fantastical Billiard

In the *Critique of Pure Reason*, Kant's response to the Humean challenge constitutes the moment of the "transcendental deduction," more precisely: the moment of the "objective deduction of the categories." It is not possible to reconstitute its details here, and I will confine myself to recalling its general strategy.[6]

---

6. In the first edition of the *Critique of Pure Reason* (1781), the objective deduction is found in the third section of chapter II. In the second

"Deducing" the categories of understanding means, in Kant's lexicon, legitimating its application to experience. This legitimation is not self-evident because the categories are "universal forms" like causality (from the same causes, the same effects always follow), while experience always presents us with particular situations. Deducing the category of causality (Kant identified eleven other categories, but we are not interested in them) amounts to resolving Hume's problem, since it is a matter of affirming that the identified causes, under the same circumstances, will universally produce the same effects. Kant thus intends to legitimate our belief in the necessity of physical laws, but he does not intend to do so in the manner of a speculative metaphysician, like Leibniz for instance. Faced with Hume's challenge, a Leibnizian would no doubt have responded that it is possible to demonstrate the existence of a wise God who set "his heart" on creating and conserving the best of all possible worlds—ours. The constancy of the world is then secured by the immutable wisdom of a sovereign Being. We know that Kant does not proceed in this way, because he generally rejects every form of speculative thought that is secured by

---

edition of the *Critique* (1787), it occupies §15 to 24 of the second chapter of chapter II—more specifically, §20-21. For a linear commentary on the objective deduction of 1781, the reader can refer to Jacques Rivelaygue, *Leçons de métaphysique allemande*, tome II (Grasset, 1992), 118-124.

an absolute truth. Instead, his strategy consists in proposing a *proof by contradiction* of the constancy of physical laws.

We can present things as follows. Hume asks: what allows us to exclude the possibility of the fantastical trajectories of billiard balls that he evokes, as a result of a pure inconstancy of physical laws? The principle of the Kantian response is the following: we will not be able to perceive, under any circumstances, this scene that we are imagining because what would make it possible—the contingency of natural laws—would also make every perception and object-consciousness impossible. In fact, if the scene of the Humean balls is imaginable as a scene, it is because the "décor," on the basis of which our balls frolic, remains eminently stable: the billiard table, the smoke-filled room where the players themselves are standing—in short the whole context of the billiard balls refutes the hypothesis of the contingency of laws. This context testifies more broadly to the persistence of a world around the balls, i.e., of a nature that has remained impeccably subject to laws. If natural laws were to fail in the case of the balls, it is because they failed in general, and thus the world itself would collapse and with it, of course, every subjective representation of this world.

According to Kant, the flaw in Hume's reasoning is thus that it dissociates the conditions of science and the conditions of consciousness. Hume, in fact, provides us with a situation in which we become aware of a world where science is impossible. A world in which we can still perceive objects—tables, balls—but objects which are doing anything whatsoever and are inaccessible to scientific theory. But for Kant, consciousness without science is the very ruin of reasoning: consciousness cannot survive the absence of science, i.e., the absence of a world that can be known scientifically. This proves the impossibility that such a collapse of science and of natural laws may *become manifest* to us one day: we will never see the Humean "billiard scene," not because it is absolutely impossible that our world would collapse one day—only a speculative metaphysician can affirm this impossibility in an absolute way—but because the collapse of this world would be *ipso facto* the collapse of every world-form as well as that of the consciousness capable of witnessing this spectacle.

Our aim is not to restore the letter of Kant's argumentation, but what we believe to be its spirit, which espouses the following gradation:

1. Let's suppose that laws stop governing the given and that objects lose their constancy. Science, then, would become impossible, but we could never perceive this; at best we might dream it. For the difference between perception and dream, according to Kant, passes uniquely—this is the consequence

of his idealism—through the difference between objects that obey physical constancies and those that do not. Since I am never dealing with things in themselves but only with representations, the difference between objective representations (fruits of my experience) and chimerical representations (fruits of my imagination) comes down to the difference between the representations ordered by the categories (thus causally ordered) and those that are not ordered by anything other than the arbitrariness of succession (reveries without a concept). If natural things ceased to obey causal connections, everything would assume the appearance of a dream, and we would not be able to affirm that we have perceived a strange phenomenon rather than dreamed or fantasized it.

This is the first stage of the argument, which can be illustrated by the famous oneiric scene of cinnabar in the subjective deduction.[7] Kant writes:

> If cinnabar were now red, now black, now light, now heavy, if a human being were now changed into this animal shape, now into that one, if on the longest day the land were covered now with fruits, now with ice and snow, then my empirical imagination would never even get the opportunity to think of heavy

7. Whereas the objective deduction establishes that the categories apply to experience, the subjective deduction examines how—by means of which faculties and operations—this application is realized.

cinnabar on the occasion of the representation of the color red.[8]

We should stress that the imaginary summoned here by Kant, at the heart of which everything takes on the consistency of a dream, is homogeneous to the imaginary mobilized by Hume in his billiard scene, namely an extro-science imaginary, an XSF imaginary. Kant, as I said, does not commit the error that Popper made: he does not mistake a problem of extro-science fiction for a problem of science fiction. He confronts Hume on his own terrain—the lawless real—and pits it against his own idea of chaos. Chaos against chaos, cinnabar against billiard: the first victim of Kantian chaos is perception, which becomes indistinguishable from phantasm.

2. But Kantian chaos will prove even more intense than that which is described in the cinnabar scene, and thus more intense than the chaos of the Humean billiard scene. For if the laws disappeared, according to Kant, the real could not even have the consistency of a dream, in which I still manage to discern things: a cinnabar that decomposes, men who are transformed into animals, a countryside that goes through all the seasons in a single day. In truth, a lawless real would even be too unstable to

8. Immanuel Kant, *Critique of Pure Reason*, trans. Paul Guyer and Allen Wood (Cambridge University Press), 229 (A. 100-101).

allow for the delineation of such entities-in-becoming: every entity would implode as soon as it was created; and nothing would have the time to differentiate itself from nothing.

3. But since every form of temporal continuity would come to be broken, I myself could not subsist, in the form of a self-consciousness capable of witnessing the spectacle of this frightening desolation, for my own memory would disappear in its turn as soon as it emerged. Everything would be reduced to the punctual and perpetually amnesiac intuition of a point of chaos without density and without relation to its past. Reality, having become as unreal as my dream, then less real than every dream, would absorb the dream of such an annihilation into its nothingness. Nothing would remain other than a pure chaotic manifold, without consciousness or consistency.

So we see that Kant's demonstration is a *factual* demonstration: since the contingency of laws, as Hume envisioned it, would imply the abolition of representation and of the world, the very fact *that there had been* representation of a world would refute the Humean hypothesis. And it is necessary to add— I will come back to this—that at the same time that this hypothesis of a contingency of physical laws is disqualified, the Kantian approach also appears to condemn in advance the extro-science imaginary as a potential literary genre. Such an imaginary seems bound to be reduced to the monotony of a pure disorder at the heart of which nothing subsists and nothing is distinguished from nothing.

b) Possibility of Non-Kantian Worlds

Nevertheless, such a remark concerning the extro-science imaginary puts us immediately on the track of a possible weakness in the Kantian solution. What prevents us, after all, from imagining extro-science worlds that are much more stable and therefore much more interesting than those described by Kant? Why, exactly, can we not imagine worlds that are not subject to necessary laws; thus worlds that are unstable, capable here or there of absurd behavior, but regular on the whole, although their regularity does not result in any way from necessary causal processes? In other words, what allows Kant to exclude the possibility of worlds that are *in fact* broadly regular, but have an *approximate* regularity, not derived from any universal law? Why should a lawless world be, without fail, frenetically inconstant?

Kant tells us: if our world did not obey any necessary law, nothing would subsist of the world. But— we want to reply to him—a world that obeyed no law has no reason to be chaotic rather than ordered: it has to be equally capable of one and the other precisely because we cannot impose limits on it. At bottom, it seems that Kant brings into play an implicit law that allows him to affirm the identity between a world without necessary laws and radical chaos: this law is a *probabilistic* law. Kant makes the following implicit argument: if a world were lawless, if the least of its parcels could behave indifferently in any way whatsoever, it would take an extraordinary chance to compose a global and durable order, like the nature that confronts us. But if this is Kant's argument, it is easy to reply to him that a world which does not obey any law has no reason to obey any probabilistic or statistical law whatever it may be. Nothing prohibits it from composing—against every sound probability— a global order that would constitute it into a world, an order at the heart of which certain details could nonetheless "run out of control" at any moment, like Hume's billiard balls. So we see that the weakness of the transcendental deduction derives from the practical insufficiency of its XSF imaginary: a more acute imagination of extro-science fiction would have prevented Kant from excluding the potentiality, either that the world in the future will be transformed into a lawless world, or even that we already live in such a world, whose chaotic details have not yet appeared in a clear way. As a result, his resolution of the Humean enigma—how to demonstrate the necessity of physical laws, their future persistence—by the transcendental deduction would not have appeared to him as satisfying as it seems at first sight.[9]

If we try in turn to deepen this hypothesis of extro-science worlds, we notice that Kant's thesis, according to which science and consciousness have the same conditions of possibility (namely, the necessity of laws), does not withstand scrutiny. For we can fiction as many worlds as we desire that clearly contradict it.

We can in fact conceive of three types of extro-science worlds, of which a single type corresponds to what Kant describes whereas the other two depart from his imaginary:

a. Worlds that we will call "type 1": these are all the possible worlds that are irregular, but whose irregularity does not affect science or consciousness. They are not extro-science worlds in the strict sense, because they still permit the exercise of science. But they are worlds that contradict the thesis according to which the strict necessity of laws is a condition for the possibility of science as well as consciousness.

These worlds would contain causeless events, yet the realization of these events would be too rare,

---

9. For a more precise version of this critique, the reader can consult *After Finitude* (Bloomsbury Academic, 2010).

too "spasmodic," to endanger science as well as consciousness. Such events would consist of observable causal ruptures, but it would be impossible to reproduce the ruptures in a regular way.

Type-1 worlds would not endanger science, for science is structurally indifferent to events that can give place only to a testimony and not to a protocol of observation. If, in this world, someone claimed to have observed an unconformable phenomenon during a few brief moments, scientists would have nothing to say about it. And this is not because they would necessarily doubt the good faith of the witness—not even because they would suppose him to be mad or the victim of a hallucination—but simply because science can do nothing about events whose observation does not obey a procedure that ensures their reproducibility. Even if testimonies multiply concerning physically improbable events, and even if we imagined a world in which these events would be physically absurd, experimental science would not—literally—care about them and would not even be jeopardized, since its proper domain—the reproducible experiments—would not be impaired by this type of chaos. For science, every phenomenon that is "punctually causeless" would either be non-existent or not yet have a demonstrable cause. Thus, it would have no consequence for science's existence.

As far as consciousness is concerned, we do not see how it would perish. The dream, the hallucination would continue to exist, and to exist as distinct from effective perceptions in which absurd phenomena would suddenly take place. Certainly, each witness to a causeless event would in principle ask himself if he has not dreamed or hallucinated, but he would have precise reasons to reject these possibilities. For in this type of world, which is broadly regular, he could consider that the context of the event is not identical to that of the dream (he would not sleep, he would not feel awake after the observation), or to that of the hallucination (in this world, the hallucination would be tied to certain identifiable pathologies). Furthermore: he could appeal, in certain cases, to the reliable criterion of intersubjectivity, for it could be that these events were produced before a multitude of witnesses, who thus guarantee for one another the fact that they have not dreamed. One would live in a universe where, alongside an unimpaired sphere of events "for scientists" (which can be reproduced at will in the laboratory), events "for witnesses" would also take place here and there, irreproducible, infrequent, and yet quite real.

Since non-causal type-1 worlds are effectively thinkable, this proves that neither science nor consciousness has as its condition of possibility the strictly universal application of the principle of causality. Both would continue to be possible in a world that has moderately departed from the principle of causality.

b. Type-2 worlds: these are the worlds whose irregularity is sufficient to abolish science, but not consciousness. They are thus genuine extro-science worlds.

In such worlds, no evental sphere would be preserved from a-causal disorder. Laboratory experiments would start in their turn to produce the most diverse results, abolishing the possibility of constituting a science of nature. But in this type of world—here is the supreme inconsistency— daily life could always build on stabilities that are certainly very relative, but still sufficiently powerful to allow a conscious existence. In this world, "accidents of things" would take place, and material objects would abruptly "swerve off the road"; these accidents would be too rare to destroy every human life but not rare enough to permit reliable scientific experimentation. A world whose margins would become capricious, but this caprice would not refer to any hidden intention. A world in which we could only *chronicle* things. We would say, for example, assuming we can use the lexicon of our own theories in that world: "from this date to that date, the nature 'of the laboratory' ceased to be relativist and regressed toward Newtonian dynamics"; or again: "from this date to that date, a genuine 'renewal' of quantum physics took place, particularly in the laboratories of the southern hemisphere," and so forth. So we can no longer extract universal—properly scientific—laws from the course of nature; we can only record variations of behavior that very diverse theories (which are valid each time for determinate times and places) can potentially describe.

But let's be precise: in truth, no manifest irregularity could ever suffice to demonstrate that a hidden law does not underlie the apparent disorder. Whatever the manifest disorder, we can always, as Bergson emphasized after Leibniz, detect an unknown order within it, or an order that does not correspond to the order we hoped for. In an extro-science world, we could thus always imagine a hidden law existing beneath the apparent disorder of natural chronicles. But in that world, those who persist in seeking such a secret law behind the absurd variations of nature would seem just as eccentric or vain as those who still try, in our own world, to find a quantitative law capable of explaining and predicting the course of human history.

In such a world, to extend the previous metaphor of "accidents of things," we would be in the midst of objects, a little like a motorist in the midst of other vehicles: we could in general rely on a reasonable behavior of the real, but we could never rule out an absurd behavior on the part of nature, in the same way we can never rule out rubbing shoulders with a driver who is disrespectful of the traffic laws. A greater vigilance would thus be the consequence of such a nature—which is capable of swerving, but is almost "regular" on the whole. The "road accidents" can thus be subjected to frequential laws, and it is upon such frequencies that our vigilance can intuitively be built, even when we do not have in mind exact percentages for the evaluation of risks. The same would be true in type-2 nature: the plausibility of real behavior would be sufficient to compile general empirical statistics in this nature, to act and live within it, although in a painfully uncertain mode—since a general frequency never excludes a devastating exception. In sum, natural regularity would be analogous to social regularity: it would be sufficiently stable to permit daily existence, but too unpredictable to give place to exact predictions or to avoid a sudden catastrophe.

But if we conceded a certain "statistical" constancy to the type-2 world, wouldn't we be implicitly acknowledging that the beginning of a science of nature (albeit one that is frequential and embryonic) is still possible? So that the analogy between the two regularities—society and type-2 nature—is more exact and enables us to think a world not subject to any experimental science, we should add a historical dimension to it. Let's suppose that a man at the end of the 18th century tried to evaluate the approximate frequency of carriage accidents in the Paris of his time. If this man had known that the number of carriage accidents in 19th century Paris would tend toward zero, he could have deduced from this fact that the process of equine safety had made an extraordinary leap from one century to the other. What he would not have foreseen is the near-total disappearance of carriages, in favor of a means of transport that was non-existent in his time. Thus social regularity, which allows us in the short and medium term to build on the quantifiable probability of the behavior of others despite its individual unpredictability, is coupled with the possibility of a historical change on the largest scale: an unpredictable change in a more profound sense, because it is impossible to subject it to any quantitative law. And yet, these epochal changes, which cannot be inscribed in experimental causal laws, did not eliminate every trace of social regularity, even at the height of historical upheavals, i.e., in the course of transitions from one era to another. Similarly, we could then say that the "men" of type-2 worlds would know "transitions between natural eras," which are tied to progressive—but radically unpredictable—transformations of daily constancies, transformations that escape every frequential study. But this time, in contrast to the causes we can potentially detect in historical change, these transformations would be *entirely* devoid of demonstrable causes: they would introduce "epochs" in nature, whose long-term modifications would be added to the "tremors of things" in the short term. In this world, causeless events would weave—outside every strict probability—shifting, strange regularities in which men, for better or for worse, would attempt to pursue their individual existence.

In short: such a nature, which is capable of marginal caprices and epochal modifications, is effectively thinkable—and with it *a disconnection between the conditions of the possibility of science and those of consciousness*. A world in which the conditions of science disappear is not necessarily a world in which the conditions of consciousness are abolished as well. Consciousness without science is not the ruin of thought.

c. Finally, the third type of universe devoid of necessary laws would no longer be a world: it would be a universe in which disorderly modifications are so frequent that, following the example of chaos described by Kant in the objective deduction, the conditions of science as well as those of consciousness would be abolished.

We thus see, among the three categories of universes we have fictioned, that two contradict the transcendental deduction and one constitutes a world engendered by extro-science fiction: type-2 world, or XSF-2 world.

This XSF-2 world has a double import. First of all, by its mere thinkability it sums up the double failure of Kant and Popper to resolve the Humean enigma: we do not know how to refute, by means of reason, the possibility that such worlds could exist. There is thus a speculative import in exhibiting the possibility of an extro-science nature, which invites us to think Hume's challenge anew. It seems clear, in fact, that the two previous attempts renew our belief in the necessity of natural laws and in their future stability. But what we nevertheless discover is that the contingency of the laws of nature is not an absurd hypothesis, i.e., it is thinkable and unrefuted (by Kant or by Popper). So what prevents us from effectively accepting this possibility? Why not accept what logic (the principle of non-contradiction) and experience (present or past) tell us in concert, namely that nothing rules out that the actual world rests on a shifting terrain which could one day yield under our feet? A third option for the resolution of our problem emerges here, which would no longer consist in establishing what cannot be established— the necessity of laws—but would consist, conversely, in establishing the *effective contingency* of natural constancies, then in confronting the major question that results from this: if the world has no necessity, how is its apparently impeccable regularity—more perfect than that of type-1 worlds—possible?

But I will not confront this problem which I treated elsewhere,[10] because my aim here is different: it is to examine the "literary" import of extro-science worlds, insofar as they do not belong to the same imaginary as science fiction. Can we conceive of XSF as a narrative genre that could compete with SF?

---

10. *After Finitude*, Chapter 4.

3. Extro-Science Fiction and Narration

Could there be, and under what conditions, XSF novels? Are there already novels of this kind, stamped with the seal of "science fiction" but which, as I have tried to show, belong in fact to another type of imaginary?

a) Three Procedures

The difficulty in elaborating XSF novels—and what seems at first sight to condemn them to constitute isolated singularities—is that we start from what normally has to be excluded from narration: not only pure arbitrariness, but an arbitrariness that can be reproduced at any moment. If the reader of science fiction is ready to grant to futuristic novels initial postulates as fanciful as possible, he requires the author to rigorously stick to these postulates and not introduce ruptures into the world he elaborated without cause or reason, which would remove all interest from the entire narration. In fact, we have to understand that if Hume's hypothesis took place in a world, then there would be events that are literally engendered *by nothing*—in other words, pure upsurges *ex nihilo*. For it is a matter of imagining a change of laws that is not itself provoked by a law or a cause of a superior order—in which case we would always be in a world governed by constancies and/or by a specific rationality: physical constancies or demiurgic, even divine rationality. Transposed into the framework of a tale, this amounts to introducing gratuitous caesuras here and there, which cannot be explained by the series of recounted events. In other words, the novice narrator's mistakes become ontologically grounded and typical of the genre. How, in this case, should we structure a story? Is there any interest in plunging into the adventures of an XSF-2 world?

First of all, let's try to understand more precisely what an XSF tale should be. It has to obey two requirements: a) within it, events take place that no real or imaginary "logic" can explain; b) the question of science is present in the tale, albeit in a negative mode. We have to be dealing with a world in which science suddenly becomes—or is in the course of becoming—impossible, either entirely or partially (in this or that chemical, physical, biological … discipline).[11] Or again, a more radical possibility: we have to present a world where science, which is always excluded because of the frequency of aberrant events, continues to haunt the universe in

_____

11. Of course it is absurd for science to "partially" survive without being affected by the destruction of one of its domains. That it subsists without subsisting as a whole is another way of saying that it has completely collapsed in its general coherence.

the manner of an absence that is intensely felt in its effects. These two traits are enough to distinguish XSF from *heroic fantasy* and from *nonsense* à la Lewis Carroll. In these two genres, science does not appear as what is lacking, because it is replaced by another logic or another regime of mastery of phenomena that saturates the tale and the situations while ensuring their intrinsic coherence: either the magic of a proto-medieval world found within *fantasy*, or that of the paradox and parody found within the *Alice* novels. XSF lacks this "heterodox continuity": it does not have a coherence of change at its disposal and instead finds itself forced to tear the tissue of its own frames through ruptures that nothing justifies, while having to compose a story with such tears.

To confront this difficulty, it seems to me that three types of solutions are possible. But my list does not claim to be exhaustive. With the help of Tristan Garcia, I have found examples of these solutions (understood as both "resolutions" and "discontinuities") in three SF tales, but only in a germinal form, since these novels—precisely because they are "science fiction" works—end each time by leading the apparently absurd events back to a rediscovered causal logic. Nonetheless, we discover in them the possibility and idea of a SF that would be progressively parasitized by XSF until the story—instead of returning to the causal bosom like the examples I will cite—would finally transition into a new literary genre.

1. The first solution amounts to introducing a single break, a unique physical catastrophe that would plunge the protagonists, overnight, into a world in which an inexplicable phenomenon is massively produced.

Robert Charles Wilson's *Darwinia* presents an initial situation of this kind: in March 1912, Europe and its inhabitants disappear overnight, leaving behind a continent of identical form but inhabited by entirely unknown flora and fauna, as an alternative product of an ancestral evolution. The event thwarts every scientific explanation, particularly the Darwinian one; hence the name "Darwinia," which is ironically applied to the new continent. But the meaning of the catastrophe is finally revealed: the Earth on which this substitution took place is not the original planet; it is an archive of this planet produced by a kind of galactic noosphere—the sum of all living beings in their most evolved state—that seeks to thicken the memory of its own past in such a way as to resist the thermic death that endangers the universe. It is this archive of the Earth that a form of machinic and malignant life attempted to violently modify in order to make it favorable to its destructive incarnation. The characters thus discover themselves to be archives with consciousnesses who have confronted the partial effacement of their own data.

2. Second solution: multiply the breaks in order to produce a form of *nonsense*, verging on the pure joke rather than governed by the subtle paradox as in Carroll. We can in fact withstand multiple arbitrary events instead of a unique catastrophe if the author takes advantage of them in order to produce absurd and unexpected situations. Type-2 worlds possess a certain *vis comica*, a certain burlesque power that can potentially be exploited.

Here we can think of Douglas Adams' *The Hitchhiker's Guide to the Galaxy*, a sort of beatnik, comic and psychedelic novel, in which we find a "generator of infinite improbability": a machine that produces at will the most absurd events and transforms missiles either into a bowl of petunias or into a sperm whale that meditates as it descends to the ground of the closest planet. But here we are dealing with a machine that is still subject to the laws of chance (it produces infinite "improbabilities"); and this generator was moreover invented by means of a reasoning that is itself probabilistic. A reasoning that, if it is in jest like the whole novel, is not any less coherent.[12]

---

12. Adams explains that scientists only knew how to produce finite-probabilities generators until a student—who was left to sweep up

Finally, this machine can be started and stopped at will, like every machine, and thus does not present a causeless, by definition unmasterable event.

3. And finally, one last possible solution: novels that take place within an uncertain reality, those in which the real would go to pieces, progressively ceasing to be familiar to us. As in the burlesque solution, the tale would multiply the breaks, but this time according to a progressive line of oppressive disintegration.

Here we can think of one of Philip K. Dick's masterpieces, *Ubik*, in which the real increasingly escapes its habitual coherence. In this novel, the characters face two series of events that are contrary to every physics and that respond to two heterogeneous "logics." On the one hand, things and beings age or regress: a phone book suddenly becomes outdated, coins that are in common use turn into coins of another era, a plant wilts as soon as it is bought, the body of young woman mummifies in one night. And on the other hand, the portrait or evocation of a recently assassinated man is found, for no reason, in aberrant places or situations: his face appears on the coins, his name is written on match boxes or

the laboratory—got the idea to calculate the finite improbability of an infinite-improbability generator. And the student in fact succeeded; as a result, he became famous and was then lynched by "respectable" physicists who were jealous of his success.

announced in television ads. This destructuration of the world creates a nightmarish atmosphere that can befit the burlesque as much as XSF-2 worlds. But once again the causal explanation of these processes intervenes. It turns out that we are dealing with the psychic world of individuals who discover that they were also assassinated; they are cryogenized half-living beings, slowly devoured by an adolescent who is himself in a coma and endowed with monstrous mental powers.

In short, we have three solutions for potential XSF novels: the catastrophe; the burlesque nonsense; the nagging uncertainty in a novel of atmosphere. But each time these extro-science beginnings are recaptured in a heterodox logic of causes and reasons, typical of SF narration.

b) An XSF prototype

I have nevertheless found a genuine XSF novel, which is mistakenly branded as science fiction; it proves by itself that such a literary genre can exist and even garner popular success: René Barjavel's *Ravage*.[13]

Like the previous examples, *Ravage* grafts itself on a SF context that it contaminates with a logic

---

13. René Barjavel, *Ravage*, Gallimard, 1996.

foreign to it. But in contrast to the three already cited novels, it is not in the end "recaptured" in a logic of causes and reasons that return it to the bosom of science fiction.

In this tale, which takes place in 2052, electricity stops existing overnight, or at least it is no longer manifest. Yet remarkably, Barjavel does not really attempt to explain the phenomenon; he merely describes its cataclysmic consequences on the Paris and France of that time as well as the way in which the hero and the main protagonists try to survive. It is true that the characters sometimes propose scientific or theological hypotheses about this disappearance (variation of sunspots or divine punishment). But nothing ever confirms their conjectures, which in any case are barely sketched out. Only the destructive effects of the event on the "High City" (a Paris dominated by immense towers) matter: conflagrations, falling aircrafts, water shortages, scenes of panic and looting. Catastrophes that extend throughout the entire country, which the narrator describes as the main characters flee far from the urban centers. Barjavel's acumen is having made the tale sufficiently breathless so that the reader has no more time or leisure to question the nature of the phenomenon than the characters themselves, who are grabbed by the throat and constantly overwhelmed by the unforeseen outcomes of the electric annihilation.

The two main speeches about this disappearance thus amount to confessions of ignorance, and propose hypotheses typical of XSF-2 worlds. The first is uttered by professor Portin, an exemplary representative of the science that had until then been celebrated, but which had now became powerless. On the street, he speaks to a crowd that recognizes him and that will trample him to death shortly thereafter under the weight of its own panic: "It is by violating all the laws of Nature and logic that electricity has disappeared. And with electricity dead, it is even more unlikely that we're alive. It's all crazy. It's an anti-scientific, anti-rational nightmare. All our theories, all our laws are overthrown."[14] The second speech is directed at the hero by doctor Fauque, who in the novel personifies a kind of "good sense" maintained at the very heart of the disaster:

> But electricity has not disappeared, my young friend. If it had vanished, we would no longer exist, we would have returned to nothing, and the universe along with us. [...] What happened is a change in the manifestations of electric fluid. [...] A caprice of nature, a warning from God? We live in a universe that we believe to be immutable because we have always seen it obey the same laws, but nothing rules out that it can abruptly start to change, that sugar become bitter and that the stone float up instead of

14. René Barjavel, *Ravage*, op. cit., p. 123.

falling when you drop it. We are nothing, my friend, we know nothing....[15]

Therefore nothing is excluded and all the hypotheses are maintained as such by these declarations, which no omniscient narrator corroborates or invalidates: either scientific aberration or "caprice of nature," which does not exclude the more profound intervention of an unknown rational order. As we said, it is in fact impossible in an XSF-2 world to formally exclude the presence of laws since, as Leibniz recalled about the sudden miracle, which apparently contradicts the idea of a Providence premeditated by God, every apparent accident under a given order is in principle compatible with the existence of a more complex order.[16] The key is that the very idea

---

15. René Barjavel, *Ravage*, op. cit., p. 151-152.
16. Leibniz can rely on this fact to maintain that the miracle does not contradict the idea of a world which has always been programmed to unwind a law that combines the greatest possible variety of phenomena with maximal order (definition of the best of possible worlds). See *Discourse on Metaphysics*, §6: "God does nothing which is not orderly and it is not even possible to imagine events that are not regular," and the example of the paper: "for everything is in conformity with respect to the universal order. This is true to such an extent that not only does nothing completely irregular occur in the world, but we would not even be able to imagine such a thing. Thus, let us assume, for example, that someone jots down a number of points at random on a piece of paper, as do those who practice the ridiculous art of geomancy. I maintain that it is possible to find a geometric line whose notion is constant and uniform, following a certain rule, such that this line passes through all

of explanation is deprived of its stakes and that the inhabitants of this world have all their time taken up by the vagaries of an environment that has become unpredictable and unrecognizable.

We know that this novel, finished in 1942 and published in 1943, painfully recalls the "return to the land" promoted by Pétain in those years. The novel is in fact steeped in a transparent ideology: the City and its gigantic towers represent a corrupt Babylonian city to which is opposed the country-side of high Provence, whose mores are still pure and from which the hero comes, who is even sad-dled with the caricature of a patronymic that sums up everything: "François Deschamps." The abolition of electricity and of its science is not presented as a univocal disaster, but on the contrary as the oc-casion of a regeneration. "Ravage" is an ambiguous title; the term never appears in the novel and can thus designate the effects of a decaying civilization as much as the earthquake of its collapse. Des-champs, at the end of an exodus leading a troop of survivors, thus returns to his native land to estab-lish a rural community in which a healthy ignorance will prevent any return to a corrupting knowledge.

---

the points in the same order in which the hand jotted them down."
G.W. Leibniz, *Philosophical Essays*, trans. Roger Ariew and Daniel Garber
(Hackett Publishing, 1989), 39.

In this sense, Barjavel's extro-science fiction results from an entire political landscape that was widespread in his time and that was hostile to science because it was hostile to the whole of modernity. I have spotted another possible reactionary source for the novel, namely Léon Daudet's *Le Stupide XIXe Siècle*. In this very well known pamphlet from 1922, the polemicist of *Action française* attacks all the conquests of the previous century, which he finds detestable—political conquests obviously, but also artistic and even scientific ones. To evaluate the science of this period, Daudet draws on the extreme resources of his bad faith and proceeds in two stages: a) science has always existed: sailing, the weaving of clothes, the making of wine and bread—in short, all the traditional techniques were already science and they have "become essential and consubstantial to civilized existence"; b) none of the discoveries of the 19th century has such a "character of durability and consubstantiality." In other words, these discoveries that are too recent have something precarious about them, because they are external to the real fundaments of our civilization. And here is Daudet's conclusion: "We feel that the science of electricity could be extinguished and disappear, by an intellectual short-circuit, like electricity itself."[17] Regardless of whether Barjavel had read this pamphlet or not, we see that the idea, and the barely masked phantasmic wish for the disappearance of modern science—symbolized by electricity—was in the air, or in a certain air, for at least twenty years.

We should not conceal the rather inglorious context in which this XSF-2 tale was produced. But we should add that a successful work always surpasses the sum of the prejudices of its era and even of its author. What makes *Ravage* more interesting as an adventure novel than its retrograde conceptions is first of all, as we said, that Barjavel never provided the reason for the cataclysm and did not interpret the phenomenon according to his ideological preferences. The possibility of science subsists, since we see at the end that a certain Denis (in reference to Denis Papin) reinvents the steam engine and is assassinated for this "crime" by Deschamps, who has become the patriarch of non-science. The possibility of knowledge also subsists, since it remains as the menace of a rediscovery of the laws of nature and thus—why not?—of electricity. That a divine punishment had taken place is not ruled out, given the biblical aspect of the narrated epic, but it is never affirmed either. And the pure "caprice of nature" also

17. Léon Daudet, *Le Stupide XIXe Siècle*, in Souvenirs *et polemiques* (Robert Laffont, 1992), 1191.

remains possible, which casts over this entire world the potential shadow of its ultimate absurdity.

Above all, this novel is remarkable because it clearly transposes onto nature itself a then-blazing historical catastrophe—the debacle of May 1940—as well as one of the upheavals that follow it: the extinguishing of lights, the black-out imposed on occupied Paris after four o'clock. This intersects with the comparison I tried to sketch out between type-2 worlds and the radicality of historical contingencies: the soft ground of the vanquished nation is transformed into the soft ground of changing nature. The political stupidity of the storyline matters little then; it cannot eliminate the originality of the tale: that it is an authentic example of XSF, a controlled tale in a world without substance.

***

So it seems that extro-science fiction can become a full-fledged genre, because it has at its disposal various procedures capable of supporting a narration despite the ambient disorder of the configured world, and above all has a real prototype that is consistent, before its time, with the requirements we have prescribed. But couldn't this genre go beyond the honorable but limited interest of adolescent fiction or adventure novels? It seems to me that we can go further: starting from traditional science fiction, we can decompose it by tilting the world toward extro-science and pursuing this enterprise of degradation toward a less and less inhabitable world, making the tale itself progressively impossible, until we isolate certain lives that are tightened around their own flow in the midst of gaps. Life mentally experiences itself without science and, in this ever more accentuated divergence, perhaps discovers something unprecedented about itself or about science. An eidetic variation pushed to the point of suffocation, self-experience in a non-experienceable world. A precarious intensity would plunge infinitely into its pure solitude, with only an environment of rubble in which to explore the truth of a worldless existence.

The Billiard Ball

by Isaac Asimov

The Billiard Ball

James Priss—I suppose I ought to say Professor James Priss, though everyone is sure to know whom I mean even without the title—always spoke slowly.

I know. I interviewed him often enough. He had the greatest mind since Einstein, but it didn't work quickly. He admitted his slowness often. Maybe it was *because* he had so great a mind that it didn't work quickly.

He would say something in slow abstraction, then he would think and then he would say something more. Even over trivial matters, his giant mind would hover uncertainly, adding a touch here and then another there.

Would the Sun rise tomorrow, I can imagine him wondering. What do we mean by "rise?" Can we be certain that tomorrow will come? Is 0 the term "Sun" completely unambiguous in this connection? Add to this habit of speech a bland countenance, rather pale, with no expression except for a general look of uncertainty; gray hair, rather thin, neatly combed; business suits of an invariably conservative cut and you have what Professor James Priss was—a retiring person completely lacking in magnetism. That's why nobody in the world, except myself, could possibly suspect him of being a murderer. And even I am not sure. After all, he was slow-thinking; he was *always* slow-thinking. Is it conceivable that at one crucial moment he managed to think quickly and act at once.

It doesn't matter. Even if he murdered, he got away with it. It is far too late now to try to reverse matters and I wouldn't succeed in doing so even if I decided to let this be published.

Edward Bloom was Priss' classmate in college, and an associate, through circumstance, for a generation afterward. They were equal in age and in their propensity for the bachelor life, but opposites in everything else that mattered.

Bloom was a living flash of light; colorful, tall, broad, loud, brash, and self-confident. He had a mind that resembled a meteor strike in the sudden and unexpected way it could seize the essential. He was no theoretician, as Priss was; Bloom had neither the patience for it, nor the capacity to concentrate intense thought upon a single abstract point. He admitted that; he boasted of it.

What he did have was an uncanny way of seeing the application of a theory; of seeing the manner in which it could be put to use. In the cold marble block of abstract structure, he could see, without apparent difficulty, the intricate design of a marvelous device. The block would fall apart at his touch and leave the device.

It is a well-known story, and not too badly exaggerated, that nothing Bloom ever built had failed to work, or to be patentable, or to be profitable. By the time he was forty-five, he was one of the richest men on Earth.

And if Bloom the Technician were adapted to one particular matter more than anything else, it was to the way of thought of Priss the Theoretician. Bloom's greatest gadgets were built upon Priss' greatest thoughts, and as Bloom grew wealthy and famous, Priss gained phenomenal respect among his colleagues.

Naturally it was to be expected that when Priss advanced his Two-Field Theory, Bloom would set about at once to build the first practical anti-gravity device.

My job was to find human interest in the Two-Field Theory for the subscribers to *Tele-News Press*, and you get that by trying to deal with human beings and not with abstract ideas. Since my interviewee was Professor Priss, that wasn't easy.

Naturally, I was going to ask about the possibilities of anti-gravity, which interested everyone; and not about the Two-Field Theory, which no one could understand.

"Anti-gravity?" Priss compressed his pale lips and considered. "I'm not entirely sure that it is possible, or ever will be. I haven't—uh—worked the matter out to my satisfaction. I don't entirely see whether the Two-Field equations would have a finite solution, which they would have to have, of course, if—" And then he went off into a brown study.

I prodded him. "Bloom says he thinks such a device can be built."

Priss nodded. "Well, yes, but I wonder. Ed Bloom has had an amazing knack at seeing the unobvious in the past. He has an unusual mind. It's certainly made him rich enough."

We were sitting in Priss' apartment. Ordinary middle-class. I couldn't help a quick glance this way and that. Priss was not wealthy.

I don't think he read my mind. He saw me look. And I think it was on his mind. He said, "Wealth isn't the usual reward for the pure scientist. Or even a particularly desirable one."

Maybe so, at that, I thought. Priss certainly had his own kind of reward. He was the third person in history to win two Nobel Prizes, and the first to have both of them in the sciences and both of them unshared. You can't complain about that. And if he wasn't rich, neither was he poor.

But he didn't sound like a contented man. Maybe it wasn't Bloom's wealth alone that irked Priss; maybe it was Bloom's fame among the people of Earth generally; maybe it was the fact that Bloom was a celebrity wherever he went, whereas Priss, outside scientific conventions and faculty clubs, was largely anonymous.

I can't say how much of all this was in my eyes or in the way I wrinkled the creases in my forehead, but Priss went on to say, "But we're friends, you know. We play billiards once or twice a week. I beat him regularly."

(I never published that statement. I checked it with Bloom, who made a long counterstatement that began "He beats *me* at billiards. That jackass—" and grew increasingly personal thereafter. As a matter of fact, neither one was a novice at billiards. I watched them play once for a short while, after the statement and counterstatement, and both handled the cue with professional aplomb. What's more, both played for blood, and there was no friendship in the game that I could see.)

I said, "Would you care to predict whether Bloom will manage to build an anti-gravity device?"

"You mean would I commit myself to anything? Hmm. Well, let' consider, young man. Just what do we mean by anti-gravity? Our conception of gravity is built around Einstein's General Theory of Relativity, which is now a century and a half old but which, within it limits, remains firm. We can picture it—"

I listened politely. I'd heard Priss on the subject before, but if I was to get anything out of him—which wasn't certain—I'd have to let him work his way through in his own way.

"We can picture it," he said, "by imagining the Universe to be flat, thin, superflexible sheet of untearable rubber. If we picture mass as being associated with weight, as it is on the surface of the Earth then we would expect a mass, resting upon the rubber sheet, to make an indentation. The greater the mass, the deeper the indentation.

"In the actual Universe," he went on, "all sorts of masses exist, an so our rubber sheet must be pictured as riddled with indentations. Any object rolling along the sheet would dip into and out of the indentations it passed, veering and changing direction as it did so. It is this veer and change of direction that we interpret as demonstrating the existence of a force of gravity. If the moving object comes close enough to the center of the indentation and is moving slowly enough, it gets trapped and whirls round and round that indentation. In the absence of friction, it keeps up that whirl forever. In other words, what Isaac Newton interpreted as a force, Albert Einstein interpreted as geometrical distortion."

He paused at this point. He had been speaking fairly fluently—for him—since he was saying something he had said often before. But now he began to pick his way.

He said, "So in trying to produce anti-gravity, we are trying to alter the geometry of the Universe. If we carry on our metaphor, we are trying to straighten out the indented rubber sheet. We could imagine ourselves getting under the indenting mass and lifting it upward, supporting it so as to prevent it from making an indentation. If we make the rubber sheet flat in that way, then we create a Universe—or at least a portion of the Universe—in which gravity doesn't exist. A rolling body would pass the non-indenting mass without altering its direction of travel a bit, and we could interpret this as meaning that the mass was exerting no gravitational force. In order to accomplish this feat, however, we need a mass equivalent to the indenting mass. To produce anti-gravity on Earth in this way, we would have to make sure of a mass equal to that of Earth and poise it above our heads, so to speak."

I interrupted him. "But your Two-Field Theory—"

"Exactly. General Relativity does not explain both the gravitational field and the electromagnetic field in a single set of equations. Einstein spent half his life searching for that single set—for a Unified Field Theory—and failed. All who followed Einstein also failed. I, however, began with the assumption that there were two fields that could not be unified and followed the consequences, which I can explain, in part, in terms of the 'rubber sheet' metaphor."

Now we came to something I wasn't sure I had ever heard before. 'How does that go?" I asked.

"Suppose that, instead of trying to lift the indenting mass, we try to stiffen the sheet itself, make it less indentable. It would contract, at least over a small area, and become flatter. Gravity would weaken, and so would mass, for the two are essentially the same phenomenon in terms of the indented Universe. If we could make the rubber sheet completely flat, both gravity and mass would disappear altogether.

"Under the proper conditions, the electromagnetic field could be made to counter the gravitational field, and serve to stiffen the indented fabric of the universe. The electromagnetic field is tremendously stronger than the gravitational field, so the former could be made to overcome the latter."

I said uncertainly, "But you say 'under the proper conditions.' Can those proper conditions you speak of be achieved, Professor?"

"That is what I don't know," said Priss thoughtfully and slowly. "If the Universe were really a rubber sheet, its stiffness would have to reach an infinite value before it could be expected to remain completely flat under an indenting mass. If that is also so in the real Universe, then an infinitely intense electromagnetic field would be required and that would mean anti-gravity would be impossible."

"But Bloom says—"

"Yes, I imagine Bloom thinks a finite field will do, if it can be properly applied. Still, however ingenious he is," and Priss smiled narrowly, "we needn't take him to be infallible. His grasp on theory is quite faulty. He—he never earned his college degree, did you know that?"

I was about to say that I knew that. After all, everyone did. But there was a touch of eagerness in Priss' voice as he said it and I looked up in time to catch animation in his eye, as though he were delighted to spread that piece of news. So I nodded my head as if I were filing it for future reference.

"Then you would say, Professor Priss," I prodded again, "that Bloom is probably wrong and that anti-gravity is impossible?"

And finally Priss nodded and said, "The gravitational field can be weakened, of course, but if by anti-gravity we mean a true zero-gravity field—no gravity at all over a significant volume of space—

then I suspect anti-gravity may turn out to be impossible, despite Bloom."

And I had, after a fashion, what I wanted.

I wasn't able to see Bloom for nearly three months after that, and when I did see him he was in an angry mood.

He had grown angry at once, of course, when the news first broke concerning Priss' statement. He let it be known that Priss would be invited to the eventual display of the anti-gravity device as soon as it was constructed, and would even be asked to participate in the demonstration. Some reporter—not I, unfortunately—caught him between appointments and asked him to elaborate on that and he said:

"I'll have the device eventually; soon, maybe. And you can be there and so can anyone else the press would care to have there. And Professor James Priss can be there. He can represent Theoretical Science and after I have demonstrated anti-gravity, he can adjust his theory to explain it. I'm sure he will know how to make his adjustments in masterly fashion and show exactly why I couldn't possibly have failed. He might do it now and save time, but I suppose he won't."

It was all said very politely, but you could hear the snarl under the rapid flow of words.

Yet he continued his occasional game of billiards with Priss and when the two met they behaved with complete propriety. One could tell the progress Bloom was making by their respective attitudes to the press. Bloom grew curt and even snappish, while Priss developed an increasing good humor.

When my umpteenth request for an interview with Bloom was finally accepted, I wondered if perhaps that meant a break in Bloom's quest. I had a little daydream of him announcing final success to *me*.

It didn't work out that way. He met me in his office at Bloom Enterprises in upstate New York. It was a wonderful setting, well away from any populated area, elaborately landscaped, and covering as much ground as a rather large industrial establishment. Edison at his height, two centuries ago, had never been as phenomenally successful as Bloom.

But Bloom was not in a good humor. He came striding in ten minutes late and went snarling past his secretary's desk with the barest nod in my direction. He was wearing a lab coat, unbuttoned.

He threw himself into his chair and said, "I'm sorry if I've kept you waiting, but I didn't have as much time as I had hoped." Bloom was a born showman and knew better than to antagonize the press, but I lad the feeling he was having a great deal of difficulty at that moment in adhering to this principle.

I had the obvious guess. "I am given to understand, sir, that your recent tests have been unsuccessful."

"Who told you that?"

"I would say it was general knowledge, Mr. Bloom."

"No, it isn't. Don't say that, young man. There is no general knowledge about what goes on in my laboratories and workshops. You're stating the Professor's opinions, aren't you? Priss', I mean."

"No, I'm—"

"Of course you are. Aren't you the one to whom he made that statement— that anti-gravity is impossible?"

"He didn't make the statement that flatly."

"He never says anything flatly, but it was flat enough for him, and, not as flat as I'll have his damned rubber-sheet Universe before I'm finished."

"Then does that mean you're making progress, Mr. Bloom?"

"You know I am," he said with a snap. "Or you should know. Weren't you at the demonstration last week?"

"Yes, I was."

I judged Bloom to be in trouble or he wouldn't be mentioning that demonstration. It worked but it was not a world beater. Between the two poles of a magnet a region of lessened gravity was produced.

It was done very cleverly. A Mossbauer Effect Balance was used to robe the space between the poles. If you've never seen an M-E Balance in action, it consists primarily of a tight monochromatic beam of gamma rays shot down the low-gravity field. The gamma rays change wave length slightly but measurably under the influence of the gravitational field and if anything happens to alter the intensity of the field the wavelength change shifts correspondingly. It is an extremely delicate method for probing a gravitational field and it worked like a charm. There was no question but that Bloom had lowered gravity.

The trouble was that it had been done before by others. Bloom, to be sure, had made use of circuits that greatly increased the ease with which such an effect had been achieved—his system was typically ingenious and had been duly patented—and he maintained that it was by this method that antigravity would become not merely a scientific curiosity but a practical affair with industrial applications.

Perhaps. But it was an incomplete job and he didn't usually make a fuss over incompleteness. He wouldn't have done so this time if he weren't desperate to display *something*.

I said, "It's my impression that what you accomplished at that preliminary demonstration was 0.82g, and better than that was achieved in Brazil last spring."

"That so? Well, calculate the energy input in Brazil and here, and then tell me the difference in gravity decrease per kilowatt-hour. You'll be surprised." "But the point is, can you reach zero g— zero gravity? That's what Professor Priss thinks may be impossible. Everyone agrees that merely lessening the intensity of the field is no great feat."

Bloom's fist clenched. I had the feeling that a key experiment had gone wrong that day and he was annoyed almost past endurance. Bloom hated to be balked by the Universe.

He said, "Theoreticians make me sick. " He said it in a low, controlled voice , as though he were finally tired of not saying it, and he was going to speak his mind and be damned. "Priss has won two Nobel Prizes for sloshing around a few equations, but what has he done with it? Nothing! I *have* done something with it and I'm going to do more with it, whether Priss likes it or not."

"I'm the one people will remember. I'm the one who gets the credit. He can keep his damned title and his prizes and his kudos from the scholars. Listen, I'll tell you what gripes him. Plain old-fashioned jealousy. It kills him that I get what I get for doing. He wants it for *thinking*."

"I said to him once—we play billiards together, you know—" It was at this point that I quoted Priss' statement about billiards and got Bloom's

74

counterstatement. I never published either. That was just trivia. "We play billiards, said Bloom, when he had cooled down, "and I've won my share of games. We keep things friendly enough. What the hell— college chums and all that—though how he got through. I'll never know. He made it in physics, of course, and in math, but he got a bare pass—out of pity, I think—in every humanities course he ever took."

"You did not get your degree, did you, Mr. Bloom?" That was sheer mischief on my part. I was enjoying his eruption.

"I quit to go into business, damn it. My academic average, over the three years I attended, was a strong B. Don't imagine anything else, you hear? Hell, by the time Priss got his Ph.D., I was working on my second million."

He went on, clearly irritated, "Anyway, we were playing billiards and I said to him, 'Jim, the average man will never understand why you get the Nobel Prize when I'm the one who gets the results. Why do you need two? Give me one!' He stood there, chalking up his cue, and then he said in his soft namby-pamby way, 'You have two billions, Ed. Give me one.' So you see, he wants the money."

I said, "I take it you don't mind his getting the honor?"

For a minute I thought he was going to order me out, but he didn't. He laughed instead, waved his hand in front of him, as though he were erasing something from an invisible blackboard in front of him. He said, "Oh, well, forget it. All that is off the record. Listen, do you want a statement? Okay. Things didn't go right today and I blew my top a bit, but it will clear up. I think I know what's wrong. And if I don't, I'm going to know.

"Look, you can say that I say that we *don't* need infinite electro-magnetic intensity; we *will* flatten out the rubber sheet; we will have zero gravity. And when we get it, I'll have the damndest demonstration you ever saw, exclusively for the press and for Priss, and you'll be invited. And you can say it won't be long. Okay?"

Okay!

I had time after that to see each man once or twice more. I even saw them together when I was present at one of their billiard games. As I said before, both of them were *good*.

But the call to the demonstration did not come as quickly as all that. It arrived six weeks less than a year after Bloom gave me his statement. And at that, perhaps it was unfair to expect quicker work. I had a special engraved invitation, with the assurance of a cocktail hour first. Bloom never did things by halves and he was planning to have a pleased and satisfied group of reporters on hand. There was an arrangement for trimensional TV too. Bloom felt completely confident, obviously; confident enough to be willing to trust the demonstration in every living room on the planet.

I called up Professor Priss, to make sure he was invited too. He was.

"Do you plan to attend, sir?"

There was a pause and the professor's face on the screen was a study in uncertain reluctance. "A demonstration of this sort is most unsuitable where a serious scientific matter is in question. I do not like to encourage such things."

I was afraid he would beg off, and the dramatics of the situation would be greatly lessened if he were not there. But then, perhaps, he decided he dared not play the chicken before the world. With obvious distaste he said, "Of course, Ed Bloom is not really a scientist and he must have his day in the sun. I'll be there."

"Do you think Mr. Bloom can produce zero gravity, sir?"

"Uh ... Mr. Bloom sent me a copy of the design of his device and ... and I'm not certain. Perhaps he can do it, if ... uh ... he says he can do it. Of course"—he paused again for quite a long time—"I think I would like to see it."

So would I, and so would many others.

The staging was impeccable. A whole floor of the main building at Bloom Enterprises—the one on the hilltop—was cleared. There were the promised cocktails and a splendid array of hors d'oeuvres, soft music and lighting, and a carefully dressed and thoroughly jovial Edward Bloom playing the perfect host, while a number of polite and unobtrusive menials fetched and carried. All was geniality and amazing confidence.

James Priss was late and I caught Bloom watching the corners of the crowd and beginning to grow a little grim about the edges. Then Priss arrived, dragging a volume of colorlessness in with him, a drabness that was unaffected by the noise and the absolute splendor (no other word would describe it—or else it was the two martinis glowing inside me) that filled the room.

Bloom saw him and his face was illuminated at once. He bounced across the floor, seized the smaller man's hand and dragged him to the bar. "Jim! Glad to see you! What'll you have? Hell, man, I'd have called it off if you hadn't showed. Can't have this thing without the star, you know." He wrung Priss' hand. "It's your theory, you know. We poor mortals can't do a thing without you few, you damned *few* few, pointing the way."

He was being ebullient, handing out the flattery, because he could afford to do so now. He was fattening Priss for the kill.

Priss tried to refuse a drink, with some sort of mutter, but a glass was pressed into his hand and Bloom raised his voice to a bull roar.

"Gentlemen! A moment's quiet, please. To Professor Priss, the greatest mind since Einstein, two-time Nobel Laureate, father of the Two-Field Theory, and inspirer of the demonstration we are about to see—even if he didn't think it would work, and had the guts to say so publicly."

There was a distinct titter of laughter that quickly faded out and Priss looked as grim as his face could manage.

"But now that Professor Priss is here," said Bloom, "and we've had our toast, let's get on with it. Follow me, gentlemen!"

The demonstration was in a much more elaborate place than had housed the earlier one. This time it was on the top floor of the building. Different magnets were involved—smaller ones, by heaven—but as nearly as I could tell, the same M-E Balance was in place.

One thing was new, however, and it staggered everybody, drawing much more attention than anything else in the room. It was a billiard table, resting under one pole of the magnet. Beneath it was the companion pole. A round hole, about a foot across, was stamped out of the very center of the table and it was obvious that the zero-gravity field, if it was to be produced, would be produced through that hole in the center of the billiard table.

It was as though the whole demonstration had been designed, surrealist fashion, to point up the victory of Bloom over Priss. This was to be another version of their everlasting billiards competition and Bloom was going to win.

I don't know if the other newsmen took matters in that fashion, but I think Priss did. I turned to look at him and saw that he was still holding the drink that had been forced into his hand. He rarely drank, I knew, but now he lifted the glass to his lips and emptied it in two swallows. He stared at that billiard table and I needed no gift of ESP to realize that he took it as a deliberate snap of fingers under his nose.

Bloom led us to the twenty seats that surrounded three sides of the table, leaving the fourth free as a working area. Priss was carefully escorted to the seat commanding the most convenient view. Priss glanced quickly at the trimensional cameras which were now working. I wondered if he were thinking of leaving but deciding that he couldn't in the full glare of the eyes of the world.

Essentially, the demonstration was simple; it was the production that counted. There were dials in plain view that measured the energy expenditure. There were others that transferred the M-E Balance readings into a position and a size that were visible to all. Everything was arranged for easy trimensional viewing.

Bloom explained each step in a genial way, with one or two pauses in which he turned to Priss for a confirmation that had to come. He didn't do it often enough to make it obvious, but just enough to turn Priss upon the spit of his own torment. From where I sat I could look across the table and see Priss on the other side.

He had the look of a man in Hell.

As we all know, Bloom succeeded. The M-E Balance showed the gravitational intensity to be sinking steadily as the electromagnetic field was intensified. There were cheers when it dropped below the 0.52g mark. A red line indicated that on the dial.

"The 0.52g mark, as you know," said Bloom confidently, "represents the previous record low in gravitational intensity. We are now lower than that at a cost in electricity that is less than ten percent what it cost at the time that mark was set. And we will go lower still."

Bloom—I think deliberately, for the sake of the suspense—slowed the drop toward the end, letting the trimensional cameras switch back and forth between the gap in the billiard table and the dial on which the M-E Balance reading was lowering.

Bloom said suddenly, "Gentlemen, you will find dark goggles in the pouch on the side of each chair. Please put them on now. The zero gravity field will soon be established and it will radiate a light rich in ultraviolet."

He put goggles on himself, and there was a momentary rustle as others went on too.

I think no one breathed during the last minute, when the dial reading dropped to zero and held fast. And just as that happened a cylinder of light sprang into existence from pole to pole through the hole in the billiard table.

There was a ghost of twenty sighs at that. Someone called out, "Mr. Bloom, what is the reason for the light?" "It's characteristic of the zero-gravity field," said Bloom smoothly which was no answer, of course. Reporters were standing up now, crowding about the edge of the table. Bloom waved them back. "Please, gentlemen, stand clear!"

Only Priss remained sitting. He seemed lost in thought and I have been certain ever since that it was the goggles that obscured the possible significance of everything that followed. I didn't see his eyes I couldn't. And that meant neither I nor anyone else could even begin to make a guess as to what was going on behind those eyes. Well maybe we couldn't have made such a guess, even if the goggles hadn't been there, but who can say?

Bloom was raising his voice again. "Please! The demonstration is not yet over. So far, we've only repeated what I have done before. I have now produced a zero-gravity field and I have shown it can be done practically. But I want to demonstrate something of what such a field can do. What we are going to see next will be something that has never been seen, not even by myself. I have not experimented in this direction, much as I would have liked to, because I have felt that Professor Priss deserved the honor of—"

Priss looked up sharply. "What—what—"

"Professor Priss," said Bloom, smiling broadly, "I would like you to perform the first experiment involving the interaction of a solid object with a zero-gravity field. Notice that the field has been formed in the center of a billiard table. The world knows your phenomenal skill in billiards, Professor, a talent second only to your amazing aptitude in theoretical physics. Won't you send a billiard ball into the zero-gravity volume?"

Eagerly he was handing a ball and cue to the Professor. Priss, his eyes hidden by the goggles, stared at them and only very slowly, very uncertainly, reached out to take them.

I wonder what his eyes were showing. I wonder, too, how much of the decision to have Priss play billiards at the demonstration was due to Bloom's anger at Priss' remark about their periodic game, the remark I had quoted. Had I been, in my way, responsible for what followed?

"Come, stand up, Professor," said Bloom, "and let me have your seat. The show is yours from now on. Go ahead!"

Bloom seated himself, and still talked, in a voice that grew more organ-like with each moment. "Once Professor Priss sends the ball into the volume of zero gravity, it will no longer be affected by Earth's gravitational field. It will remain truly motionless while the Earth rotates about its axis and travels about the Sun. In this latitude, and at this time of day, I have calculated that the Earth, in its motions, will sink downward. We will move with it and the ball will stand still. To us it will seem to rise up and away from the Earth's surface. Watch."

Priss seemed to stand in front of the table in frozen paralysis. Was it surprise? Astonishment? I don't know. I'll never know. Did he make a move to interrupt Bloom's little speech, or was he just suffering from an agonized reluctance to play the ignominious part into which he was being forced by his adversary?

Priss turned to the billiard table, looking first at it, then back at Bloom. Every reporter was on his feet, crowding as closely as possible in order to get a good view. Only Bloom himself remained seated, smiling and isolated. He, of course, was not watching the table, or the ball, or the zero-gravity field. As nearly as I could tell through the goggles, he was watching Priss.

Perhaps he felt there was no way out. Or perhaps—

With a sure stroke of his cue, he set the ball into motion. It was not going quickly, and every eye followed it. It struck the side of the table and caromed. It was going even slower now as though Priss himself were increasing the suspense and making Bloom's triumph the more dramatic.

I had a perfect view, for I was standing on the side of the table opposite from that where Priss was. I could see the ball moving toward the glitter of the zero-gravity field and beyond it I could see those portions of the seated Bloom which were not hidden by that glitter.

The ball approached the zero-gravity volume, seemed to hang on the edge for a moment, and then was gone, with a streak of light, the sound of a thunderclap, and the sudden smell of burning cloth.

We yelled. We all yelled.

I've seen the scene on television since—along with the rest of the world. I can see myself in the film during the fifteen-second period of wild confusion, but I don't really recognize my face.

Fifteen seconds!

And then we discovered Bloom. He was still sitting in the chair, his arms still folded, but there was a hole the size of a billiard ball through forearm, chest, and back. The better part of his heart, as it later turned out under autopsy, had been neatly punched out. They turned off the device. They called in the police. They dragged off Priss, who was in a state of utter collapse. I wasn't much better off, to tell the truth, and if any reporter then on the scene ever tried to say he remained a cool observer of that scene, then he's a cool liar.

It was some months before I got to see Priss again. He had lost some weight but seemed well otherwise. Indeed, there was color in his cheeks and an air of decision about him. He was better dressed than I had ever seen him to be.

He said, "I know what happened *now*. If I had had time to think, I would have known then. But I am a slow thinker, and poor Ed Bloom was so intent on running a great show and doing it so well that he carried me along with him. Naturally, I've been trying to make up for some of the damage I unwittingly caused."

"You can't bring Bloom back to life," I said soberly.

"No, I can't," he said, just as soberly. "But there's Bloom Enterprises to think of, too. What happened at the demonstration, in full view of the world, was the worst possible advertisement for zero-gravity, and it's important that the story be made clear. That is why I have asked to see *you*."

"Yes?"

"If I had been a quicker thinker, I would have known Ed was speaking the purest nonsense when he said that the billiard ball would slowly rise in the zero-gravity field. It *couldn't* be so! If Bloom hadn't despised theory so, if he hadn't been so intent on being proud of his own ignorance of theory, he'd have known it himself.

"The Earth's motion, after all, isn't the only motion involved, young man. The Sun itself moves in a vast orbit about the center of the Milky Way Galaxy. And the Galaxy moves too, in some not very clearly defined way. If the billiard ball were subjected to zero gravity, you might think of it as being unaffected by any of those motions and therefore of suddenly falling into a state of absolute rest—when there is no such thing as absolute rest."

Priss shook his head slowly. "The trouble with Ed, I think, was that he was thinking of the kind of zero-gravity one gets in a spaceship in free fall,

87

when people float in mid-air. He expected the ball to float in mid-air. However, in a spaceship, zero-gravity is not the result of an absence of gravitation, but merely the result of two objects, a ship and a man within the ship, falling at the same rate, responding to gravity in precisely the same way, so that each is motionless with respect to the other.

"In the zero-gravity field produced by Ed, there was a flattening of the rubber-sheet Universe, which means an actual loss of mass. Everything in that field, including molecules of air caught within it, and the billiard ball I pushed into it, was completely massless as long as it remained within it. A completely massless object can move in only one way."

He paused, inviting the question. I asked, "What motion would that be?"

"Motion at the speed of light. Any massless object, such as a neutron or a photon, must travel at the speed of light as long as it exists. In fact, light moves at that speed only because it is made up of photons. As soon as the billiard ball entered the zero-gravity field and lost its mass, it too assumed the speed of light at once and left."

I shook my head. "But didn't it regain its mass as soon as it left the zero-gravity volume?"

"It certainly did, and at once it began to be affected by the gravitational field and to slow up in response to the friction of the air and the top of the billiard table. But imagine how much friction it would take to slow up an object the mass of a billiard ball going at the speed of light. It went through the hundred-mile thickness of our atmosphere in a thousandth of a second and I doubt that it was slowed more than a few miles a second in doing so, a few miles out of 186,282 of them. On the way, it scorched the top of the billiard table, broke cleanly through the edge, went through poor Ed and the window too, punching out neat circles because it had passed through before the neighboring portions of something even as brittle as glass had a chance to split a splinter.

"It is extremely fortunate we were on the top floor of a building set in a countrified area. If we were in the city, it might have passed through a number of buildings and killed a number of people. By now that billiard ball is off in space, far beyond the edge of the Solar System and it will continue to travel so forever, at nearly the speed of light, until it happens to strike an object large enough to stop it. And then it will gouge out a sizable crater."

I played with the notion and was not sure I liked it. "How is that possible? The billiard ball entered the zero-gravity volume almost at a standstill. I saw it. And you say it left with an incredible quantity of kinetic energy. Where did the energy come from?"

Priss shrugged. "It came from nowhere! The law of conservation of energy only holds under the conditions in which general relativity is valid; that is, in an indented-rubber-sheet universe. Wherever the indentation is flattened out, general relativity no longer holds, and energy can be created and destroyed freely. That accounts for the radiation along the cylindrical surface of the zero-gravity volume. That radiation, you remember, Bloom did not explain, and, I fear, could not explain. If he had only experimented further first; if he had only not been so foolishly anxious to put on his show—"

"What accounts for the radiation, sir?"

"The molecules of air inside the volume. Each assumes the speed of light and comes smashing outward. They're only molecules, not billiard balls, so they're stopped, but the kinetic energy of their motion is converted into energetic radiation. It's continuous because new molecules are always drifting in, and attaining the speed of light and smashing out."

"Then energy is being created continuously?"

"Exactly. And that is what we must make clear to the public. Anti-gravity is not primarily a device to lift spaceships or to revolutionize mechanical movement. Rather, it is the source of an endless supply of free energy, since part of the energy produced can be diverted to maintain the field that keeps that portion of the Universe flat. What Ed Bloom invented, without knowing it, was not just anti-gravity, but the first successful perpetual-motion machine of the first class—one that manufactures energy out of nothing."

I said slowly, "Anyone of us could have been killed by that billiard ball, is that right, Professor? It might have come out in any direction."

Priss said, "Well, massless photons emerge from any light source at the speed of light in any direction; that's why a candle casts light in all directions. The massless air molecules come out of the zero-gravity volume in all directions, which is why the entire cylinder radiates. But the billiard ball was only one object. It could have come out in any direction, but it had to come out in some one direction, chosen at random, and the chosen direction happened to be the one that caught Ed."

That was it. Everyone knows the consequences. Mankind had free energy and so we have the world we have now. Professor Priss was placed in charge of its development by the board of Bloom Enterprises, and in time he was as rich and famous as ever Edward Bloom had been. And Priss still has two Nobel Prizes in addition.

Only....

I keep thinking. Photons smash out from a light source in all directions because they are created at the moment and there is no reason for them to move in one direction more than in another. Air molecules come out of a zero-gravity field in all directions because they enter it in all directions.

But what about a single billiard ball, entering a zero-gravity field from one particular direction? Does it come out in the same direction or in any direction?

I've inquired delicately, but theoretical physicists don't seem to be sure, and I can find no record that Bloom Enterprises, which is the only organization working with zero-gravity fields, has ever experimented in the matter. Someone at the organization once told me that the uncertainty principle guarantees the random emersion of an object entering in any direction. But then why don't they try the experiment?

Could it be, then....

Could it be that for once Priss' mind had been working quickly? Could it be that, under the pressure of what Bloom was trying to do to him, Priss had suddenly seen everything? He had been studying the radiation surrounding the zero-gravity volume. He might have realized its cause and been certain of the speed-of-light motion of anything entering the volume.

Why, then, had he said nothing?

One thing is certain. *Nothing* Priss would do at the billiard table could be accidental. He was an expert and the billiard ball did exactly what he wanted it to. I was standing right there. I saw him look at Bloom and then at the table as though he were judging angles.

I watched him hit that ball. I watched it bounce off the side of the table and move into the zero-gravity volume, heading in one particular direction.

For when Priss sent that ball toward the zero-gravity volume—and the tri-di films bear me out—it was already aimed directly at Bloom's heart!

Accident? Coincidence?

... Murder?

Univocal Publishing
123 North 3rd Street, #202
Minneapolis, MN 55401
univocalpublishing.com

ISBN 9781937561482

Jason Wagner, Drew S. Burk
(Editors)

This work was composed in
Berkley and Block.

All materials were printed and bound
in April 2015 at Univocal's atelier
in Minneapolis, USA.

The paper is Hammermill 98.
The letterpress cover was printed
on Crane's Lettra Flourescent.
Both are archival quality and acid-free.